KOJO OWUSU-ANSAH

THE RIGHT FOUNDATION

A book for everyone who desires a glorious destiny

Foreword by Evans Darko-Mensah

Copyright 2011

Revised Edition 2020
Kojo Owusu-Ansah

All rights reserved. No part of this publication may be reproduced, stored in a retrievable system, or transmitted in any form or by any means, electronic, mechanical, photocopy, recording or otherwise without a prior permission of the publisher.

P.O Box BT 535
Tema
Tel: +233545309992
Email: kowusuansah@gmail.com, frykoo2004@gmail.com

Editing by: Samilia Eshun
Email: samiliad@yahoo.com
Mobile: +233 20 024 6954

Designed and Printed by: Kobina Eshun
Email: Kobina.eshun@gmail.com
Mobile: +233 24 495 2487

<u>Dedication</u>

To the Holy Spirit,
who has been my source of inspiration and
guidance, all these years in Christ Jesus.
I really appreciate your love to me Holy Spirit.

Table of Contents

Acknowledgement

My sincere gratitude to the Almighty God for his grace and mercies to even write this book. My admiration as well to the General Overseer of Life International Church, the associate Pastors and the entire leadership of the church.

I am also grateful to Mr. and Mrs. Akpe, the Ackon family, the Owusu-Ansah family and Mr. Gabriel Anderson. I love you and may the Lord continually make all your efforts successful!

My thanks also to Mr. Evans Darko-Mensah, Mr. Anuwa-Amah, Mr. Richard Cobbinah and Rev. Reginald Adanuvo who have contributed in various ways to the making of this book.

Thanks to all past and present executives and members of Legon Pentecostal's Union (A Generation of Power) for the opportunity given me to serve the Lord on campus. Being a part of this Union has really impacted my life greatly.

Thanks also to my loyal friends and all who have been a source of inspiration to me – Maxwell Arthur, Prince Tetteh, Emmanuel Gbedemah, Elisha Kitcher, Senyo Ahu, Dodzi Apkakli, Richard Mensah (Political), Josephine Cobbinah, Akushika Burnside, Prosper Nartey, Sylvester Siaw, Edna Wilmax, roommates, study mates, and colleagues at church. I really appreciate your love to me. May your foundation continually be in the Lord Jesus.

<u>Foreword</u>

Amazing Grace! Abundant grace! It is by grace we have been saved through faith and it is the same grace that will enable us live victorious, glorious Christian life. It is my privilege to be invited to write a foreward to this book – the fruit of the labours of a dedicated soldier of the Lord.

To know our Lord Jesus Christ, to experience Him personally and to make Him known among all people, is among the highest callings of God on every child of God. The surest ways of getting to know our Lord Jesus Christ intimately are through personal devotion, bible study and meditation, prayer and above all, walking in obedience to the Word.

These are the main topics discussed in this book by Kojo Owusu-Ansah, a fine young man who loves the Lord and is energised by a deep sense of mission to his peers. The Bible says, 'How can a young man cleanse his way? By taking heed to according to your Word" Psalm 119:9 (NKVV).

I therefore recommend this book to its intended target group… the Youth in Christ. I pray that it may help keep themselves pure and undefiled for the Lord. I also hope that the adults may see in it the hope of the generations and may the Lord Jesus Christ Himself bless his enterprise. To the Glory of God the Father. "…Christ in you, the hope of Glory." Col. 1:27 (b)

Evans Darko-Mensah
Life International Church
Faith Chapel, Tema

God requires us to live in every day as if Christ is coming and also work out our salvation with fear and trembling.
Brother Kojo Owusu-Ansah, through the inspiration of the Holy Ghost teaches us on how we can build our daily relationship with God and to discover who we are in Christ. I therefore recommend this book since it touches on such issues.
Moses Bentil
(Former President, Legon Pentecostals' Union. University of Ghana)

In fact, this book "THE RIGHT FOUNDATION" is really a foundation for greatness and through it my eyes are enlightened. What I like about this book is the simplicity with which these principles are shared. They are straightforward and easy to understand. Grab a copy now, read it yourself and you'll surely testify to it.

Bro. Richard Donkor
Former President, University Christian Fellowship
University of Ghana, Legon

<u>Introduction</u>

As a young graduate of University of Ghana, it came to a time that I became very sad in my spirit on campus, due to the fact that some colleagues who had inspired me in the Lord in Senior High School have now backslidden. I contemplated about this for some time and later asked the Lord about it. What I heard from the Lord was that those colleagues were not rooted and grounded in Him. This caused me to put these materials together as a book to help you not to miss your place in Christ Jesus.

Please do not expect this book to flow like other books since is a compendium of articles and messages I have preached before. It is an easy book to read and in a form of a study.

I have used quite a number of different Bible translations to help you understand what I truly want to communicate since some of the translations are easy to understand. Take your Bible along as you read and make every scripture part of your life and you will experience that transformation in Christ Jesus and also, cause you to be rooted and grounded in Him.

Below is a summary of the various chapters in the pages of this book.

Chapter 1 – The Right Foundation: explains some of the bases on which your life needs to stand on in order to soar higher in life.

Chapter 2 – Daily Walk With God: explains how one can have

a meaningful relationship with God and the benefits that go with it.

Chapter 3 – The Value Of The Soul: is to make you realise the need to give your life to Jesus Christ if you have not and also to see the need to reach out for soul winning.

Chapter 4 – Friendship: gives the understanding of being friends with the right people after you have accepted Jesus Christ as your Lord and personal saviour in order not to jeopardise your Christian life.

Chapter 5 – Determine Your Limit: expounds on 3 fundamental issues in the life of Joseph. These are (1) He refused to listen to her (2) He refused to be with her and (3) He refused to sleep with her. These issues are to help you maximise your Christian Life.

Chapter 6 – Who I Am In Christ: this chapter outlines essential scriptures of who you are in Christ. These scriptures if contextualised in your Christian life will cause you to be rooted and grounded in Christ.

Chapter 7 – Fundamental Prayer Topics: outlines some prayer topics that will be of tremendous help to you on your threshing floor. You must bring God in remembrance to His word in prayers, so use the scriptures for the right prayer topics for maximum results even as the Holy Spirit leads and directs you in prayers.

Every foundation not prescribed in scriptures is fake. The Holy

Spirit enlightens you even as you read through the pages of this book. Stay blessed!

May the Holy Spirit enlighten you even as you journey through the pages of this book.

Amen!

Chapter 1
THE RIGHT FOUNDATION

According to the Oxford dictionary of Current English the word Foundation means an underlying basis for something. This chapter explains some of the basis on which your life needs to stand on in order to soar higher in life. Every high-rise building looks attractive, but the strength that keeps it in place lies in its foundation. Likewise, every attractive life you find today in Christianity has a sure foundation, grounded and strong, right down to the depth of the heart. On the other hand, every shameful Christian you see today is a victim of shallowness in foundation.

"Anyone who listens to my teachings and obeys me is wise, like a person who builds a house on solid rock. Though the rain comes in torrents and the floodwaters rise and the winds beat against that house, it won't collapse, because it is built on rock. But anyone who hears my teaching and ignores it is foolish, like a person who builds a house on sand. When the rains and floods come and the winds beat against that house, it will fall with a mighty crash."

Matthew 7:24-28 (NLT)

From these scriptures there are some important things that we need to take notice of:
    a. Listening
    b. Obedience
    c. Building
    d. Storms

Jesus made it clear that to begin the journey of greatness, one needs to listen to his word and obey it. In Joshua 1:8, God told Joshua that, "Study this book of the Law continually. Meditate on it day and night so you may be sure to **obey** all that is written in it. Only then will you succeed."

Jesus likened the one who obeys him as one who builds his house on a rock. Building a house on a rock requires great effort and strength. One needs to cut through the rock and lay the foundation. The foundation may include iron rods, sand, stone, cement, water and other materials as well. The cost involved is very great. Jesus, therefore, implied that obeying him is not on a silver platter. It will really take great effort - endurance, perseverance, and pains because digging through a rock is not easy. However, the good news is: "I have been crucified with Christ and I no longer live, but Christ lives in me. The life I live in the body, I live by faith in the son of God, who loved me and gave himself for me." Galatians 2:20

Christ now lives in you, his nature is in you. In fact, your weakness (disobedience) can encourage you to put your trust in Christ who lives within you, instead of trusting in yourself by recognising the presence of Christ in you. You are certainly a new creation if you have given your life to Jesus Christ, but you are still a weak human being compared with the might and power of Christ. So you have to trust in Him instead of yourself for His life in you to be expressed in every situation you find yourself in order to obey him.

Any time you obey God, you are building on the right foundation for your future. Presently, it may seem you are a fool. Remember, the beginning of a whole thing does not matter but the end thereof. On the television, one is likely to see very tall and beautiful buildings especially in Europe. The height of such buildings is determined by its foundation. Obeying the Words of Jesus is a sure promise that you are going to rise to greater heights in life. The question is, "how high do you want to go in life?"

For your academics to take you somewhere, the word of God says in 2 Timothy 2:15a, "Study to show thyself approved unto God." If you obey this Word and study you will always see yourself on top of your class and will excel in all your examinations, therefore, you will see yourself rising from JHS to SHS to the tertiary institution. If God says pay your tithe and I will rebuke the devourer for your sake and you obey him, you will see your business always at the top. God will lift up a standard against anything that will bring your business down.

As children of God, the Bible says in Ephesians 6:1-2(NLT) "Children, obey your parents because you belong to the Lord, for this is the right thing to do. Honour your father and mother; this is the first of the ten commandments that ends with a promise. And this is the promise: If you honour your father and mother, "you will live a long life, full of blessings." Amen.

Most teenagers find it difficult to obey their parents. They accept the approval of friends more than what their parents tell them. At times it takes a very long time to obey a simple instruction given to them by their parents. For your information, delayed obedience is disobedience. The foundation in this scripture is the guarantee of a long life. The word of God is full of simple instructions; do this, don't do that, go here, don't go there and many others. As you begin your journey on a daily walk with God you will discover many of such scriptures in the word of God.

In as much as you obey your parents; you have to obey your siblings, teachers and colleagues whose advice are biblical and do not lead to destruction. The right foundation you lay today will determine the future you build, which will distinguish you from your colleagues and the rest of the world.

Some right foundations you can lay from today:

1. The Foundation of Prayer:

Prayer is communication between you and God based on the knowledge of God's words. Prayer is the weapon that makes you successful in all of life. EM Bounds said, "Prayer blesses all things, brings all things, believes all things and prevents all things". He said the other time also in his book *"The weapon of prayer"*, that "Failure to pray is failure in all of life and nothing is done well without prayer for the simple reason that it leaves God out of the work." Jesus' ability to reveal the Father through what He said and did came out of His relationship with the Father. The same will be true of us – our ability to reveal Christ through what we say, and so will come out of our relationship with Him. Prayer builds and strengthens that relationship that enables us to become sensitive to the voice of His Spirit. (2Chron 7:14, Luke 18:1, Eph 1:16-18, Eph 3:16-17, Phil 1:19, Col 1:9, 2Thes 3:1, 2, 1Jn 5:14-15, Job 22:27)

2. The Foundation of Reading and the study of God's word:

The word of God is the LIFE by which we are to live our lives. The Bible says, "those who know their God shall be strong and do exploits"(Dan 11:32) not those who cry or weep to God. It is through the Word that God reveals Himself. The Word of God appropriated and expressed in our lives leads us into a deeper understanding of God, greater faith, victories over temptations and a deeper prayer time.
(Ps 119:11, Ps 119:103, Ps 119:116, Josh 1:8, Matt. 4:4, Luke 1:38, 2Tim 3:16, Heb. 4:12, 1Pet 2:8)

3. Foundation of Character:

Gal 5:22 "But when the Holy Spirit controls our lives, He will produce this kind of fruit in us: love, joy peace, patience, kindness, goodness, faithfulness, gentleness and self-control. Here there is no conflict with the law." The life of Christ in you, when allowed to expression will show forth these fruit of His Spirit which is a sure foundation for exploits. Remember, Jesus said that in your flesh life, our self-life, there is nothing good.

So your flesh cannot reflect the person or the character of God, no matter how hard you try but to simply trust in Christ in you to express his life. The fruit of the Spirit is a sure foundation for our lives wherever we go. Faithfulness in Ghana is accepted as faithfulness in the UK, America and everywhere for such there is no conflict with the law.
(1John 3:11-24, 1John 4:7-8, Neh 8:10, Ps 34:14, Prov. 3:3, Heb. 6:12, Rom. 14:17, Luke 16:10)

4. Foundation of Trust:

Trusting is showing your commitment to the Word of God no matter the situation you find yourself in. It is to say "if God doesn't do it, my position remains the same." This is the work God requires of us, to trust in Jesus Christ, God's Son, the One He sent, who now lives in us in the power of His Spirit! He will always do what is right in the best possible way! Of course, He is expressing His life in and through us, so the results will always be far better than to trust in our human factor. Colin Urquhart said, "This is the key to successful living: not to trust yourself, even in your strong abilities, but to stand to one side so the Christ In you can express His life through you." Trusting serves as the foundation on which we see victories in our lives. (Ps 125:1, Ps 118:8-9, Ps 112:7, Jer 17:5 & 7, Ps 34:8 & 22, 2 Chronicles 13:18, 1 Tim 6:17, Pro 3:5, Pro 28:25)

5. Foundation of Righteousness:

Proverbs14:34 (NIV) "Righteousness exalts a nation, but sin is a disgrace to any people". The exaltation is dependent on the foundation of righteousness. Is important to note that God has made Christ our Righteousness (1 Cor 1:30) and when Christ who lives in us expresses his life through us, he will help us believe right and do right things to bring glory to His name. (Eph 6:14, Isa 62:1, Dan 12:13)

6. Foundation of Preparation:

By believing right that the plans God has for you are of good and not of evil, to give you a hope and a future enables you to prepare towards it (Jer 29:11). In 2 Chronicles 27:6 the Bible says, "So Jotham became mighty because he prepared his ways before the Lord his God." Preparation is the platform for promotion. No institution or person is honoured without preparation. Joseph prepared Egypt towards 7 years of famine and the whole land of Egypt became Pharaoh's. Begin now to prepare towards the future God has planned for you; for it is the right foundation that you are laying for a greater future. (Gen 41:47-49, Pro 16:9, Pro 21:5,31, 1 Chron 22:5, Esther 2:17, Job 22:28)

7. Foundation of Mentorship:

Beloved, there is nothing new under the sun. In whatever purpose God has given you, others have attained commanding heights in it before. Know what those successful people did in any area of your purpose and repeat those processes over and over until you get the same or better results. It is said that, "the secret of successful people is in their stories". God recommends mentorship and it is only through that that we attain to quality leadership. Mentorship is a sure foundation for the maximisation of your purpose. (Heb 6:12, 2 Chr 26:5, 1 Kings 19:19-21)

8. Foundation of Capacity Building:

Capacity is the ability to contain or the ability to perform a given task skillfully. If one performs a given task on common sense one is likely to obtain a common result, for the skills that one applies to the task is what brings out the difference between common result and an extraordinary result. It is imperative to note that true capacity is in "Christ in you" (Col 1:27). Christ overcame, was victorious and triumphant.

Allow Him to express His life in you and you'll obtain extraordinary results. In Exodus 31:1-3 (NLT), The Lord said to Moses, "look I have chosen Bazalel son of Uri, grandson of Hur, of the tribe of Judah, **I have filled him with the Spirit of God**, giving him great wisdom, intelligence, and skill in all kinds of crafts." Note that the **Spirit of God** giving him great wisdom, intelligence and skill were the capacity God gave Bazalel to carry out his work. The vision or purpose God has for you in life is seen as a building. The right knowledge and materials you need to fulfill it is the capacity which serves as the right foundation for that purpose. (See also, 1 King 4; 29-34, Dan 1:17)

9. Foundation of Discipline:

Bishop David O. Oyedepo in a leadership empowerment summit in Ghana defined discipline as an asset of inestimable value, that is, efficient management of your time, energy and resources in a bid to delivering your mandate. The efficient management of one's time, energy and resources serves as the right foundation to fulfill your purpose, vision or mandate in life. George Verwer, founder of Operation Mobilisation said, "I learned from Billy Graham that unless you are ready for a disciplined life then forget your Christian commitment.

Discipline means doing what you know you should do rather than what you feel like doing."
(Prov 6: 4- 10, Mk 1:35)

10. Foundation of Obedience:

Obedience is what guarantees you the blessings of God. Your success in life is based on your obedience to the commands of God. Put God's word into practice; for it is a Word to obey and not just to listen to and your faith in God will be strengthened. Jesus said, "whoever has my commands and obeys them, he is the one who loves me…" (John 14:21). So obedience is ultimately the outward expression of our love for Jesus Christ. It also enables him to reveal himself to us and since every revelation leads to elevation, is a sure foundation for upliftment.
(Deut 28:1, 1Sam 15:22, Eph 6:1, Matt 7:24, Phil 2:8, Acts 5:29, Rom 13:1, Rom 12:25, Ps 119:9, Pro 6:20, Heb 2:1)

From the passage in Matthew 7:24-28 the second person Jesus mentioned also heard the word of God but paid no heed to it. He assumed such people as those who build their house on the sand and when the rains and the winds come, brings it down.

Disobedience leads to shallow foundations. Normally it is the easy life, that is doing what you think is best for you even when is contrary to the Word of God or what your parents tell you. "Everybody is doing it so why don't I do it?" This statement has lured a lot of young people into ungodly lifestyles and ungodly relationships. Today you may not see the effect but some few years to come you'll see the horror you've done to yourself.

In the Bible, Sampson's parents told him not to marry any

Philistine woman but he thought he was on top of everyone, even the Word of God concerning his life. As he chose his own way it led him to his untimely death. This is very clear that disobedience leads to untimely death.

Jesus made it clear that whatever you do in life you are building a foundation and a house as well. How high do you want your building to be? A ground floor, storey building or a tower? No one can build it for you, is all in your hands. What foundations are you laying for the future?

Lastly, Jesus made it clear that the rains, floods, and winds will come against that house and those who have shallow foundations are the ones who will suffer. The rains, floods and winds are the issues or storms of life that will confront everyone in life. Currently, we hear of economic hardships in the form of credit crunch, high petroleum prices and increases in goods and services. Those with shallow foundations have given in to adultery, sexual immorality, prostitution, armed robbery and other bad social vices to pay for bills simply because they cannot stand on their foundation which is shaking.

May this not be said of you. That is why this book is for you. To help you choose the right foundation through Christ in you which is your hope. So that at the end you'll come out as the head and not the tail, the first and never the last.

Because of God's special favour to me, I have laid the foundation like an expect builder. Now others are building on it. But whoever is building on this foundation must be very careful. For no one can lay any other foundation than the one we already have - Jesus Christ. Now anyone

who builds on that foundation may use gold, silver, jewels, wood, hay or straw. But there is going to come a time of testing at the judgment day to see what kind of work each builder has done. Everyone's work will be put through the fire to see whether or not it keeps its value.
1 Corinthians 3: 10-15

Apostle Paul made it known that Jesus is the one and only foundation that can be laid. In John 1:1, 14 Bible says, "In the beginning the word already existed. He was with God, and He was God. So the word became human and lived here on earth among us. He was full of unfailing love and faithfulness. And we have seen his glory, the glory of the only Son of the father."

Jesus is introduced as the Word of God and that means the foundation is also the Word of God. Jesus himself said, "Anyone who listens to my teachings and obeys me is wise, like a person who builds a house on solid rock."

Apostle Paul made mention that there will be a time of testing, where everyone's work will pass through the fire to see if it will keep its value. This was exactly what Jesus said about the rains, floods, and winds. In academic education, there is always a time of testing where everyone is tested. There are always those who come out as the first in class and those who come out as the last. The difference between these people is that "all other things being equal" one studied and the other person did not.

There is always a time of testing in life and for a victorious success you need Jesus. He is the word that you need to lay that right foundation. I am giving you the opportunity today to accept Jesus as your Lord and personal saviour. Kindly say this prayer after me.

Dear God, I accept your son Jesus Christ as my Lord and personal saviour. I am sorry for my sins. Please have mercy on me and cleanse me from all unrighteousness. Come and stay in my heart today and make me a new creation. Please express your nature through me. I thank you for accepting me as your child in the mighty name of Jesus. Amen.

Chapter 2
DAILY WALK WITH GOD

"I am the true vine, and My Father is the vinedresser. Every branch in Me that does not bear fruit He takes away. And every one that bears fruit, He prunes it so that it may bring forth more fruit. Now you are clean through the Word which I have spoken to you. Abide in Me and I in you. As the branch cannot bear fruit of itself unless it remains in the vine, so neither can you, unless you abide in Me. I am the vine, you are the branches. He who abides in Me, the same brings forth much fruit; and I in him, for without Me you can do nothing. If anyone does not abide in Me, he is cast out as a branch and is withered. And they gather and cast them into the fire, and they are burned. If you abide in Me, and My words abide in you, you shall ask what you will, and it shall be done for you. In this My Father is glorified, that you bear much fruit; so you will be My disciples. John 15:1-8{NKJV}

From this scripture, Jesus represents himself as the true vine, the Father as the gardener and you and believers as the branches.

Branches are always joined to the vine and what flows through the vine passes through the branches.

Jesus said if you remain in me and I remain in you, you will be fruitful. The question is how do I remain in Jesus in order to be fruitful? This brings us to having a daily walk with God, which is often referred to as devotion or quiet time.

Quiet time simply means, a serene place and period set aside between you and God for fellowship. You speak to God and He also speaks to you through his word. The fellowship becomes enjoyable when you have with you a Bible and a devotional guide (eg. Daily Power or a Daily Bread) which will help you benefit from anointed teachers whose ministry will help you grow in the Lord. Not limiting yourself to the devotional guide but opening your spirit to what the word of God has for you.

<u>Principles to Quiet time</u>

1. Recognise and activate the presence of the Holy Spirit.
2. Ask the Holy Spirit to give you revelation, illumination and understanding as you read the Word of God.
   "Open my eyes, so that I may behold wonderful things out of your Law" Psalm 119:18
   That the God of our Lord Jesus Christ, the Father of glory, may give to you the spirit of wisdom and revelation in the knowledge of Him: The eyes of your understanding being enlightened; that ye may know what is the hope of His calling, what the riches of the glory of His inheritance in the saints,... Eph 1:17-18
3. Savour God's word to you and ask yourself these

questions:

    a. What's the meaning of the scripture I read?

    b. What does it mean in my circumstance?

    c. What did I not understand?

    d. What did I learn about God?

    e. What should I do?

    f. Is there a command, prayer, promise or what is it in the word for me to obey?

4. What phrase of scripture can I take with me today?

5. Write down whatever the Lord tells you.

6. Spend some time in intercessory prayers- for yourself, family, church, nation and any other prayer request the Lord lays on your heart and develop the habit of waiting to hear what God will speak to you through His Spirit. There are things God needs to tell you directly through His Spirit.

7. Thank God for his Word and commit every activity of the day into God's hands.

The time spent should not be a problem but the issue should be whether you had a fellowship with God. Jesus gave us a good example while on earth. "And rising up quite early in the morning, He went out and went away into a deserted place, and He was praying there". (Mark 1:35) He had a fellowship (He agreed with the Father and obeyed the Father) with the Father, and that was the number one secret of his success while on earth.

Henry Ward Beecher once said, "The first hour is the rudder of the day. This is often called the "golden hour" it is the hour in which you programme your mind and set your emotional tone for the rest of the day. If you set up in the morning at least two hours before you have to be at work or before your first appointment and spend the first hour investing in your mind-taking in "mental protein" rather than "mental candy", reading good books rather than the newspaper or magazines-your whole day will flow more smoothly. You'll be more positive and optimistic. You'll be calm, more confident and more relaxed. You'll gain a greater sense of control and well-being by the very act of reading healthy material for the first hour of each day.

Benefits of Quiet time {Devotion}

1. It brings us closer to the father. James 4:8a (NLT) "Draw close to God and God will draw close to you."

2. It enlightens us about God and gives us notice about what God doesn't like. Psalm 119:18 says "Open my eyes to see the wonderful truths in your Law."

3. It enables us to bear fruit. John 15:4 says "Remain in me, and I will remain in you. For a branch cannot produce fruit if it is severed from the vine, and you cannot be fruitful apart from me".

4. It enables us to encourage ourselves through the presence of God. 1 Sam 30:6 (KJV) says, "And David was greatly distressed; for the people spoke of stoning him, because the soul of all the people was grieved, every man for his sons and for his daughters: but David encouraged himself in the LORD his God.

5. It brings us into favour with God and people. Gen 39:2 "The Lord was with Joseph and blessed him greatly as he served in the home of his Egyptian master."

6. It reveals the inner thoughts of our heart. (See Psalm 51).

7. It brings us success. 1 Sam 18:14 says, "David continued to succeed in every thing he did, for the Lord was with him." 2 Chronicles 26:5 also says, "Uzziah sought God during the days of Zachariah, who instructed him in the fear of God. And as long as the king sought the Lord, God gave him success.

8. It gives us the confidence to trust the Lord by presenting our prayer request to him. Psalm 34:17 "The Lord hears his people when they call to him for help. He rescues them from all their troubles."

9. A relationship with the Lord helps to express the life of Christ in us. Gal 2:20 "I have been crucified with Christ and I no longer live, but Christ lives in me. The life I live in the body, I live by faith in the son of God, who loved me and gave himself for me."

10. It gives us the strength to stand against temptations. 1Cor 10:13 "But remember that the temptations that come your way are not different from what others experience. And God is faithful. He will keep the temptation from becoming so strong that you can't stand up against it. When you are tempted, he will show you a way out so that you will not give in to it."

From the passage read earlier on in John 15:1-8 we got to know that each one of us is a branch, producing some level of fruitfulness.

- No fruit
- Fruit
- More fruit
- Much fruit

The fruit Jesus mentioned represents good works- a thought, attitude of ours that God values because it glorifies him. It also represents best results or a sweetest price in life. In Ephesians 2:10 Bible says, "For we are his workmanship, created in Christ Jesus for good works, which God prepared before hand that we should walk in them."

God had already planned that you should bear fruit in Him and one journey of discovery that will bring fruitfulness is having a quality time with God, which happens to be the most important relationship of your life. In this relationship you seek, long for, thirst for, wait for, see, know, hear, love and respond to a person. More quality time with God means more of him in your thoughts, desires, actions and decisions.

The first level we saw was **No fruit**. These are Christians who don't fellowship with the father and for that matter their lives are not fruitful.

Jesus said his Father "takes away" every branch that bears no fruit. The words "take away" in Hebrew is "naw-saw". It implies to expiate sin - away with, bear (up), carry, lift up, loose, put away or remove. In Greek (ah'ee-ro) it also connotes to lift, by implication to take up or away. Bible even describes Jesus as the Lamb of God who "takes away" the sins of the world.

Jesus therefore implied that if you don't bear fruit or abide in him sin gets easy access into your life therefore he intervenes to take it away- Sin (uncleanness) from your life.
Since you are part of him the "take away" comes in the form of discipline to make you clean and bring you back on the right path. In Deut 8:5 (GNB) bible says, "Remember that the LORD your God corrects and punishes you just as parents discipline their children". See also (Heb 12:5-8; Job 34:31; Job 34:32; Pro 19:18; Pro 22:15; Pro 23:13; Pro 23:14; Pro 29:15; Pro 29:17; Act 14:22)

The second level of fruit bearing is **fruit**. As one begins to fellowship with the Father his or her life becomes fruitful and it becomes evident in his or her attitude and thoughts.

The third level Jesus talked about is **more fruit**. More fruit comes about as a result of pruning. Even, fruitful branches, for further fruitfulness have need of purging or pruning. In Greek, pruning is "kathairei"- taketh away (some notions, passions or humours) which hinders its growth and fruitfulness. Christ has promised to do this by His Word, and Spirit, and providence; and these shall be taken off by degrees in the proper season. From the Collins Gem dictionary pruning also means to cut off excessive branches from a tree or plant. The purging of fruitful branches, in order to increase their greater fruitfulness, is the care and work of the great vinedresser, for his own glory.

The Father prunes your life to bear more fruit. For instance in the life of Apostle Peter, after the death of Jesus he went back to fishing leaving the main work God had planned for him. But when Peter had a fellowship with Jesus his life was pruned from fishing into caring for the lambs of God. See John 21. Also, Paul's job, position, heritage, pride, and religion were also pruned away. See (Phil 3:7-8, 13-14)

The fourth level which is **much fruit** is in connection with more fruit. As we continue our fellowship with the Father, our *"more fruit"* grows into much fruit.

In John 15:6 Jesus said "If anyone does not abide in Me, he is cast out as a branch and is withered. And they gather and cast them into the fire, and they are burned". This is a description of the fearful state of hypocrites that are not in Christ.

Firstly, they are **cast out** as dry and **withered** branches. Those that abide not in Christ shall be abandoned by him; they are left to themselves, to fall into scandalous sin, and then are justly cast out of the communion of the faithful.

Secondly, men **gather** them. Satan's agents and emissaries pick them up, and make an easy prey of them. Those that fall off from Christ presently fall in with sinners; and the sheep that wander from Christ's fold, the devil stands ready to seize them for himself. When the Spirit of the Lord had departed from Saul, an evil spirit possessed him.

Thirdly, they **cast them into the fire**; that is, those who seduce them and draw them to sin do in effect cast them into the fire;

for they make them children of hell. Fire is the fittest place for withered branches, for they are good for nothing else.

Lastly, **they are burned**; this follows of course, because to be put in a fire is to be burnt. It added very emphatically, and makes the threatening very terrible.

If you profess that you are a Christian and don't spend quality time with God in fellowship you are only deceiving yourself. For you to know someone you need to spend time with the person and if you don't spend time with him at the end Jesus will simply reply to you "I don't know you" (Matt 25:12)
Don't be like Peter whom the scripture recorded (Luke 22:54) that he followed at a distance.

Peter was sharp.
He kept his distance from Jesus.
"I'll stay close enough to see him," Peter
reasoned. "But not too close, or I may get caught."

Good thinking, Peter.
    Don't get too involved – it might hurt.
    Don't be too loyal – you might get branded.
    Don't show too much concern – they'll
    crucify you too.

Peter learned a lesson that day – a hard lesson.
    It is better to have never followed Jesus
    than to have followed him and denied him.

Mark these words

Follow at a distance and you'll deny
the Master. Period.
You won't die for a man you can't touch. Period.
But stay near to him, in his shadow…
You'll die with him, gladly."

<u>Prayer</u>

Dear Lord, your word has come to me today. I see the earnest need to have a fellowship with you from today. As I begin my walk with you, please reveal yourself to me through your Word and help me by your Holy Spirit to know you more and more. Gratefully, in the mighty name of Jesus. Amen

Chapter 3
The Value of the Soul

The Longman Active Study Dictionary defines soul as the part of a person that is believed to exist even after the body has died. This is true as David said in Psalm 16:10 that, "For you will not leave my soul among the dead".

This chapter on the value of the soul is to make you realise the need to give your life to Jesus Christ and also, to reach out for soul winning.

The value of the soul can be measured on these three things.

1. Who gave it to you?

Bible makes us understand that, "And the LORD God formed man of the dust of the ground, and breathed into his nostrils the breath of life; and man became a living soul." (Gen 2:7)
It is so clear that God created us and gave us the soul. Deuteronomy 6:5 says, "And you must love the Lord your God

with all your heart, all your soul and all your strength.

2. What is the cost of it?

As a result of sin we were separated from God. God had to purchase us back again from the enemy just as 1 Cor 6:20 says, "for God bought you with a high price".

Jesus has removed us from sin; it will be painful if you are in this lost world of sin. For God so loved the world that he gave his only begotten son, that whosoever believeth in Him should not perish but have everlasting life (John 3:16). For what shall it profit you if you gain the whole world and lose your soul? Is anything worth more than your soul? (Matt 16:26). Because of you he was wounded and crushed for your sins. He was beaten that you might have peace. He was whipped, and you were healed! (Isaiah 53:5). Beloved, it caused him so much; therefore don't be enslaved by the world. (1Cor 7:23)

3. What is the effect if you lose it?

After all Jesus has done for you, if you want to live in sin and enjoy all the pleasures in this world, I announce to you that there is a place called HELL and a place called HEAVEN. There is no middle ground you can lay, for if you are hot be hot and if you are cold be cold.

The effect of losing the soul is hell and you can lose the soul if you don't accept Jesus as your Lord and personal saviour and walk in His ways.

For if you confess with your mouth that Jesus is Lord and believe in your heart that God raised him from the dead, you will be saved. For it is by believing with your heart that you are made right with God, and it is by confessing with your mouth that you are saved. Romans 10:9-10

Today if you want your sins to be forgiven and your soul to be saved, please say this prayer after me.

<u>Prayer</u>
Dear God, I come before you as a sinner. I believe in my heart that you sent Jesus to save me from my sins. Today forgive me of my sins, wash me by the blood of Jesus and take me back to you as your child. I declare that you are my Lord, Saviour and Redeemer. Thank you for forgiving me of my sins. Gratefully, in the name of Jesus. Amen

Beloved, after praying this prayer it is very important that you desire the sincere milk of the Word that you grow in the Lord (1 Peter 2:2). Chapter two of this book will help you in this regard. As a Christian, note that souls are very precious to God and until you evangelise there is no way sinners will be saved. There are two things God will never do for you as a Christian. (1) To pray for what he has already done and (2) to pray for what He has told you to do. God has told you to share His Good News and there is no way God will do that for you.

For this reason, I have explained ten reasons you should evangelise and after reading these reasons and you're not stirred to evangelise then I believe you should re-dedicate your life to Christ once more.

10 REASONS YOU SHOULD EVANGELISE
Then Jesus said unto them again, Peace be unto you: as my Father has sent me, even so send I you. John 20:21

1. It shows your gratitude to God.
We live in a world where people forget easily and so God told the Israelites through Moses that, "When you have eaten your fill, praise the LORD your God for the good land he has given you. "But that is the time to be careful! Beware that in your plenty you do not forget the Lord your God and disobey his commands, regulations and laws.

For when you have become full and prosperous and built fine houses to live in, and when your flocks and herds have become very large and your silver and gold have multiplied along with everything else, that is the time to be careful. Do not become proud at that time and forget the Lord your God, who rescued you from slavery in the land of Egypt." Deuteronomy 8:10-14

Beloved, until becoming born again we were slaves to the devil and now by the grace of God we have been set free. Colossians 1:13
Unfortunately, we forget the cruel details of the agonising sacrifice Christ made on our behalf. Familiarity breeds complacency. Even before his crucifixion, the son of God was stripped naked, beaten until almost unrecognisable, whipped, scorned and mocked, crowned with thorns and spat on contemptuously, abused and ridiculed by heartless men, He was treated worse than an animal.

Then, nearly unconscious from blood loss, he was forced to

drag a cumbersome cross up a hill, was nailed to it, and was left to die the slow excruciating torture of death by crucifixion. While his life blood drained out, hecklers stood by and shouted insults, making fun of his pain and challenging his claim to be God.

Next as Jesus took all of mankind's sin and guilt on himself, God looked away from that ugly sight, and Jesus cried out in total desperation. "My God, my God, why have you forsaken me?" Jesus could have saved himself – but then he could not have saved you.

Have your prosperity, fine homes, silver and gold caused you to forget what Jesus did for you? Please change your heart and share the Good News to a lost soul.

2. It is a command from God

And then he told them, "Go into all the world and preach the Good News to everyone everywhere." Mark 16:15
Personally, at times I reflect on the Supremacy of God. I just imagine the entire universe with the planets, stars etc. and then centre on the planet earth whereby a single of the countless stars in heaven is bigger than planet earth. That notwithstanding, I imagine the continent Africa, locate Ghana, Greater Accra Region, and then Tema and finally, imagine myself in my home and then I realise how insignificant I am. If God should tell me to carry out a task why then do I need to refuse. He is with us even till the end of age. Evangelise!

3. For the salvation of souls

But how can they call on him to save them unless they believe in him? And how can they believe in him if they have never heard about him? And how can they hear about him unless someone tells them? And how will anyone go and tell them without being sent? That is what the Scriptures mean when they say, "How beautiful are the feet of those who bring good news!" Romans 10:15

Beloved, Christ has commanded us to go (Mark 16:15) therefore, you and I have no excuse. Let's share the Good News in order for souls to be saved.

4. It helps to fulfill God's vision

God's vision is to reconcile people to himself through Christ Jesus and we are the ones to carry that mandate out. Many at times we become reluctant in carrying out this vision. Deborah and Barak son of Abinoam song records.

But in the tribe of Reuben
there was great indecision.
Why did you sit at home among the sheep folds —
to hear the shepherds whistle for their flocks?
In the tribe of Reuben there was great indecision.
Gilead remained east of the Jordan.
And Dan, why did he stay home?
Asher sat unmoved at the sea shore, remaining in his
harbors. Judges 5:15b – 17

Are you also indecisive in the decision to win souls? or why are you unmoved or like Dan do you also choose to stay at home? Rise up beloved, and speak the Word to a soul. Are you afraid that someone might insult you? Or perhaps they will laugh at you and reject the message? Yours is to be obedient and share

the Good News.
"But Zebulun risked his life, as did Naphtali, on the battlefield." Judges 5:18

Let your life count for God and he will surely reward you.

5. It is an addition to your life's purpose on earth
All this newness of life is from God who brought us back to himself through what Christ did. And God has given us the task of reconciling people to him. 2 Corinthians 5:18
Evangelism or soul winning adds to one's life purpose. We often find ourselves asking, where are we from? What are we doing here? And where are we going from here? Nonetheless, Jesus said I am from the Father, I came to do the Father's will and I'm going to the Father. That implies that we are also here to do the Father's will which includes evangelism.

6. It serves as a platform for the gifts of God in you to gain expression
"And the disciples went everywhere and preached, and the Lord worked with them, confirming what they said by many miraculous signs." Mark 16:20
Miracles mostly follow the great commission of evangelism. It will be difficult to realise the treasures deposited in you if you remain reluctant to evangelise the Word. God will always confirm His Word with signs and wonders so share the Good News.

7. It enables God to give us our heart desires
"You didn't choose me. I chose you. I appointed you to go and produce fruit that will last, so that the Father will give you

whatever you ask for, using my name." John 15:16

There are quite a number of people who claim every good thing in life by using the name of Jesus. It is important to know that every blessing comes with a responsibility. Jesus said you need to bear fruit and whatever you ask the Father in His name he will give it to you. Take up that responsibility of evangelism and enjoy the privileges of calling on God using the name of Jesus.

8. It helps to grow the church

"Those who believed what Peter said were baptised and added to the church – about three thousand in all." Acts 2:41

It is significant to know that the good news we share greatly increases the kingdom of God.

You may not have the opportunity to speak to such a large crowd of people as Peter did. Nonetheless, a soul is equally important, as the Holy Spirit works through you to share His Word. There is no need to be shy of the message, for it is the power of God unto salvation (Rom 1:16). Your weakness is of no excuse, it is Christ at work through you, therefore evangelise.

9. It forms part of your social responsibility

Most successful individuals or organisations normally donate items to enhance the development of society. These donations are important but cannot guarantee safety within our society and also eternity to the beneficiaries.

The most powerful weapon on the earth is to preach the gospel. It is only through the gospel that crime, immorality, armed robbery, "*sakawa*", etc reduces in a society. You may not have a lot of money to give to society but your obedience and humility to share the Good News can save a soul, reduce crime, immorality, transform society and bring about love and peaceful coexistence. You will agree with me beloved that this inestimable value of soul winning and its accrued benefits is of a greater social responsibility than what one donates physically. The power is in you. Arise! Share the Good News about Jesus.

10. It justifies you of guilt
"But if the watchman sees the enemy coming and doesn't sound the alarm to warn the people, he is responsible for their deaths. They will die in their sins, but I will hold the watchman responsible." Ezekiel 32:6

You are the watchman God is talking about. Sound the alarm of the gospel for the salvation of souls. Why remain silent, nonchalant, heartless and unconcerned about soul winning? Should it always be about you, your family and your job? Arise! Arise!! The time is shorter than you think. Sound the alarm beloved or else they will die in their sins and you'll be accountable.

"When the watchman sees the enemy coming, he blows the alarm to warn the people. Then if those who hear the alarm refuse to take action – well, it is their own fault if they die. They heard the warning but wouldn't listen, so the responsibility is theirs. If they had listened to the warning, they could have saved their lives."
Ezekiel 33:3-5

Prayer

Dear God, I thank you for your word today. Let your grace continually abound towards my life to do the work of evangelism. Gratefully, in Jesus' mighty name. Amen

Chapter 4
FRIENDSHIP

Two people can accomplish more than twice as much as one; they get a better return for their labour. If one person falls, the other can reach out and help. But people who are alone when they fall are in real trouble.

Ecclesiastes 4: 9-10(NLT)

Do not be yoked together with unbelievers. For what do righteousness and wickedness have in common? Or what fellowship can light have with darkness? What harmony is there between Christ and Belial? What does a believer have in common with an unbeliever? What agreement is there between the temple of God and idols?

For we are the temple of the living God. As God has said: "I will live with them and walk among them, and I will be their God, and they will be my people." "Therefore come out of them and be separate, says the Lord. Touch no unclean thing and I will receive you." "I will be a father to you, and you will be my sons and daughters, says the Lord Almighty."

2 Cor 6:14-18(NIV)

From the earlier scriptures in Ecclesiastes we got to know that two people are better than one, for they get a better return for their labour. The issue is, what kind of person are you teaming up with? For not all partners have the grace of God for the two of you to get better results. I often find it sad when I see new believers still teaming up with old friends who are not Christians and after a while return to their old ways and lifestyles.

In 2 Corinthians we got to know that it does not please the Lord for us to be yoked together with unbelievers. For instance, when you see two bulls plowing, you realise that the farmer pairs two bulls of equal strength; for when one is strong and the other is weak, the weak bull will suffer since the strong bull will pull it by its strength to plow.

Likewise, if you are standing on a table and someone who is stronger or of equal strength than you is on the ground and you try to pull the one on the ground to the table where you are whiles he also tries to pull you to the ground where he is. It is obvious that you'll fall to the ground simply because it is easier to fall from the height you are than for him to be where you are.

In the same instance, God has taken you from the kingdom of darkness into the kingdom of his dear Son Jesus Christ (see Col 1:13). What this denotes is that you are now set apart from the world amid its evil deeds to the kingdom (rule) of his dear Son

Jesus(see Matt 15:19, 1Jn 2:15-17). When you accepted Jesus as your personal saviour you became a new born baby in Christ (1 Pet 2:2) and your unbelieving friends can pull you from the place He the Lord has placed you on the table and hinder the seed of newness in you to grow.

Now that you have surrendered your life to Jesus and chosen to forsake the ungodly ways, please do not be deceived "for bad company corrupts good manners" (1 Cor 15:33). The bad companies are not only ungodly friends, but also things you choose to be around with - books, films, websites, music, etc. Proverbs 4:23 says, "Above all else guard your heart, for it affects every thing you do".

To guard your heart simply means to be careful the sort of information that gets into your spirit. For instance, ungodly music about sex can influence you into fornication. Most people think music has no capacity or ability to draw them from their fellowship with the Lord. A believer should be selective when it comes to music, especially when the author is not a Christian.

God always encourages us to be in friendship. In Proverbs 27:17 Bible says, "As iron sharpens iron, a friend sharpens a friend." As a believer you need a friend who will sharpen you up in the word of God, prayer, and also able to correct you whenever you are wrong. For a wound from a friend is better than many kisses from an enemy. (Prov 27:6)

Don't forsake a Christian friend simply because you disagreed with the person on an issue. Jesus said, "Therefore if you offer your gift on the altar, and there remember that your brother has anything against you leave your gift there before the altar and go. First be reconciled to your brother, and then come and offer your gift." (see Matt 5:23-24). David and Jonathan were such good friends that even after the death of Jonathan, his son Mephibosheth found favour in the eyes of David and stayed in the King's palace (see 2 Sam 9).

You can go very far in life if you have godly friends. Likewise, a glorious future can also be sabotaged by ungodly friends.

I remember in Secondary School, now High School, how innocent we were when we arrived on campus. For the juniors our outfits were white shirt and a white trouser or shorts, which meant everything about you should be righteous.
However, before completion some colleagues had given in to drugs, others became womanisers, some were suspended, and others were dismissed for one reason or the other.

And I believe this situation is not different from other High Schools (see 1 Cor 10:13). The root cause of most of the bad behaviours was from the type of friends those people chose. Those friends influenced their lives negatively.

If you are a young person in school or about to enter college or in the house please be wise in your decision in choosing friends. Ask God to help you choose the right people for there are "friends" who destroy each other, but a real friend sticks closer than a brother and whoever walks with the wise will become wise; whoever walks with fools will suffer harm. (Prov 18:24, Prov 13:20).

There are some Christian brothers and sisters who are very prayerful but that does not mean they are going to be good friends to you. In SHS, I remember there were *"Odjascious"* Christian brothers who were praying almost everywhere but some took their main assignment (books) in college lightly and it affected them greatly. Pastor Gordon Kisseih puts it this way, "God will not do by a miracle what you have to do by obedience."

One thing you should also note is that a false balance is abomination to the Lord: but a just weight is his delight." (Prov 11:1). Keep the right balance in all your Christian activities and you will always find yourself at the top and not beneath.

Again, in college during Speech and Prize giving day, all the awards went to Christian executives who served in the various denominations on campus and I wasn't left out as well.

I became the best Economics student in my second year even as the President of the Scripture Union, Vice President of Assemblies of God campus ministry and the chaplain of Elliot House. With God all things are possible!

One thing my father always tells me is to keep up with relationships. The fact that you are separated from a friend does not mean you should avoid being in tourch with that person. Search out for that person and stay connected, for the miracle you may be looking for is in the hands of that person. Stay connected!

<u>Prayer</u>

Dear Lord, I thank you for the friends and people you have brought into my life. Always lead me to the right people who can add positively to my life and help me to know you as the only true friend who sticks closer than a brother. Gratefully, in the mighty name of Jesus. Amen.

Chapter 5
<u>DETERMINE YOUR LIMIT</u>

And after these things it happened that his master's wife cast her eyes upon Joseph. And she said, "Lie with me." But he refused and said to his master's wife, "Behold, my master does not know what is in the house with me, and he has given all that he has into my hand. There is none greater in this house than I. Neither has he kept back anything from me except you, because you are his wife. How then can I do this great wickedness, and sin against God?" And it happened as she spoke to Joseph day by day, that **he did not listen to her to lie with her, or to be with her.** And it happened about this time that he came into the house to do his work. And none of the men of the house were inside. And she caught him by his robe, saying, "Lie with me." And he left his robe in her hand and fled, and got out. Genesis 39:7-12

The scripture talks to us about what happened between Joseph and Potiphar's wife. Bible tells us that she kept putting pressure on him day after day demanding to have sex with him.

I remember telling a colleague this story and all he could say was that Joseph *"lose guard"* meaning he should have taken up the *"scholarship"*. As we continue you will see how wise Joseph was.

There are some few things we can learn about what happened between Joseph and Potiphar's wife.

1. He refused to listen

As a child of God, who do you listen to? Joseph being wise refused to listen because he knew the consequences of listening to Potiphar's wife.
He would have given in to sex easily if he had listened to her. In our societies these days what are some of the things we should refrain from listening to?

Bible says in Psalm 149:3-4 that, "Let them praise his name in the dance: let them sing praises unto him with the timbrel and harp. For the LORD taketh pleasure in his people: he will beautify the meek with salvation." Indeed the Lord delights in the praise of his people. Music has a great effect on us. It is inspirational, helps in worship, creates an atmosphere, and also has the power to influence. Profane music has become a menace in our society these days. As a child of God if you really want to grow in Christ it will be good if you avoid listening to such music. Bible tells us (1 Cor 6:19) that our body is the temple of the Holy Spirit. If profane songs cannot be played or sang in the Church how much more our body where the Holy Spirit dwells?

Unfortunately, many Christians do not know the effect that music has on evil spirits. These are four biblical accounts which warn us about playing with the wrong music.

1. Satan, once Lucifer, was created to worship God. Music was actually ingrained in him when he was formed. Lucifer was created with tabrets and pipes. Since he fell, this gift of music has been corrupted and used to fight against God. Every Christian should be careful of secular music no matter how harmless it appears. Christian musicians must not play secular music if they want to be truly spiritual.

    Thou hast been in Eden the garden of God; every precious stone was thy covering, the sardius, topaz, and the diamond, the beryl, the onyx, and the jasper, the sapphire, the emerald, and the carbuncle, and gold: the workmanship of thy tabrets and of thy pipes was prepared in thee in the day that thou was created.
    Ezekiel 28:13 (KJV)

2. When King Saul was tormented by an evil spirit, instrumental music was used to drive away the demons.

    But the Spirit of the Lord departed from Saul, and an evil spirit from the Lord troubled him. And Saul's servants said unto him, "Behold now an evil spirit from God troubleth thee. Let our lord now command thy servants, which are before thee, to seek out a man, who is a cunning player on the harp: and it shall come to pass, when the evil spirit from God is upon thee, that he shall play with his hand, and thou shalt be well." And Saul said unto his servants, provide now a man that can play well, and bring him to me. Then said one of the servants, "Behold, I have seen a son of Jesse the Bethlehemite, that is cunning in playing, and a mighty valiant man, and a man of war, and prudent in matters, and a comely person, and the Lord is with him".

Wherefore, Saul sent messengers unto Jesse, and said, "send me David thy son, which is with the sheep." And Jesse took an ass laden with bread, and a bottle of wine, and a kid, and sent them by David, his son unto Saul. And David came to Saul, and stood before him: and he loved him greatly; and he became his armourbearer. And Saul sent to Jesse, saying, "Let David, I pray thee, stand before me; for he hath found favour in my sight. And it came to pass, when the evil spirit from the Lord God was upon Saul, that David took an harp, and played with his hand: so Saul was refreshed, and was well, and the evil spirit departed from him." 1 Samuel 16:14-23 (KJV)

Dear Friend, if music can drive away evil spirits, surely it is able to attract them too. Be careful of what you listen to because it may attract evil spirits to your life. Much of the unspiritual gospel songs are charged with evil spirits and one needs to be careful. People are charged with spirits of lust and violence when they listen to certain kind of music.

You say, "I am allowed to do anything" – but not

everything is helpful. You say, "I am allowed to do anything" – but not everything is beneficial.
1 Cor 10:23 (NLT)

3. When Elisha needed to hear from the Spirit of God, he called for the minstrel. As the minstrel played, the Spirit of God came upon him and he prophesied.

    "Elisha replied, "As surely as the Almighty lives, whom I serve, I would not bother with you except for my respect of King Jehoshaphat of Judah. Now bring me someone who can play the harp." While the harp was being played, the power of the LORD came upon Elisha, and he said, "This is what the LORD says: "This dry valley will be filled with pools of water!" 2 Kings 3:14-16
    (NLT)
    Surely, this testimony must teach you something: The right music can attract the presence of God!

4. When the musicians in the temple played instruments and worshipped God, the presence of God filled the house.

    "The trumpeters and singers performed together in unison to praise and to give thanks to the LORD. Accompanied by trumpets, cymbals, and other instruments, they raised their voices and praised the LORD with these words: "He is so good! His faithful love endures forever!" At that moment a cloud filled the Temple of the LORD. The priests could not continue their work because the glorious presence of the LORD

filled the Temple of God."
2 Chron 5:13-14 (NLT)

The presence of the Lord filled the Temple because musicians and singers were doing the right thing. Surely we must learn from this account that the right kind of instrumental music will bring in the presence of God.

God also wants us to be selective when it comes to friends because they can influence us. For instance, in 2 Samuel 13 there was a conversation that happened between Amnon and Jonadab. Jonadab gave Amnon a bad advice to pretend to be sick and later sleep with her sister. Bible also says in 1Cor 15:33 that "bad company corrupts good manners"

Friendship is good (Eccl 4:9) the type of friend is what matters, as there are friends who destroy each other (Prov 18:24).

2. He refused to be with her

Joseph refused to be with her as he kept out of her way as much as possible because to be with her would have ended up in a different thing. Proverbs 5:7-9 warns us not even to go near the door of an immoral woman but run from her as Joseph did wisely with Potiphar's wife. 1 Tim 2:22 also warns us to run from anything that stimulates youthful lust. The command here is to flee or run from immorality; anything apart from that will be dangerous. Sampson thought that being the strongest man there was no way he could fall but Delilah made him fall. Pornographic websites, bad friends, musical influences on sex, ungodly relationships can also make you fall. Be wise!

3. He refused to lie with her

Joseph refused to lie with her because he knew the power of purity. God said he will bring ruin on anyone who destroys his temple (1Cor 3:16-17). Bible continues to say that we become one with anyone that we have sex with (See 1Cor 6:15-18).

There is a great reward for keeping your virginity for Bible says that, "blessed are those who are pure in heart for they shall see God."(Heb 12:14) The Psalmist also said, "Was it for nothing that I kept my heart pure and kept myself from doing wrong? (Ps 73:13)

Don't be deceived by anyone; for when Joseph kept himself pure he became what the Lord had planned for him, which was the Prime minister of Egypt but when Sampson went to sleep with Delilah he couldn't perform all of God's assigned purpose for his life and it resulted in death. It's not enough to avoid fornication and adultery but also to keep your heart from lusting (see Matt 5).

Solomon said, "Run from her! Don't go near the door of her house! If you do you will lose your **honour** and hand over to merciless people everything you have **achieved** in life. Strangers will obtain your **wealth,** and someone else will enjoy the **fruit of your labour.** Afterward you will groan in anguish when disease consumes your body, and you will say how I hated discipline! If only I had not demanded my own way! Oh, why didn't I listen to my teachers? Why didn't I pay attention to those who gave me instruction? I have come to the brink of utter ruin, and now I must face public disgrace. " (Prov 5:8-14 NLT)

What is it that you're going to listen to, to be with and to lie with? I put this challenge before you today. "Beloved, be on guard. Stand true to what you believe. Be courageous. Be strong". (1 Cor 16:13)

Purity will help you gain honour, achievements, wealth and enjoy the fruit of your labour. Share this good news to your friends and God will richly bless you.

Finally, my brothers, whatever things are true, whatever things are honest, whatever things are right, whatever things are pure, whatever things are lovely, whatever things are of good report; if there is any virtue and if there is any praise, think on these things.
(Phil 4:8 KJV)

<u>Prayer</u>
Dear Lord, I thank you for your word, please help me to make the right choices when it comes to any material that will influence my life, since bad company corrupts good manners. Gratefully, in the mighty name of Jesus. Amen.

Chapter 6
<u>WHO I AM IN CHRIST</u>

D_{r.} Neil T Anderson, in his book *Who I Am in Christ* and *Walking in Freedom* outlined the following scriptures as a foundation to our Christian faith and I see it as a necessary material to understand the basis of one's Christian faith. Read the following scriptures and contextualise it in your life. It will cause you to live a victorious Christian life any day, anytime and anywhere.

<u>I am Accepted in Christ</u>

I am God's child
Yet to all who received him, to those who believed in his name, he gave the right to become children of God. John 1:12

I am Christ's friend
I no longer call you servants, because a servant does not know his master's business. Instead, I have called you friends, for everything that I learned from my Father I have made known

to you. John 15:15
I have been justified
Therefore since we have been justified through faith, we have peace with God through our Lord Jesus Christ... Romans 5:1

I am united with the Lord and one with Him in Spirit
But he who unites himself with the Lord is one with him in spirit. 1 Corinthians 6:17

I have been bought with a price, I belong to God
...you were bought with a price. Therefore honour God with your body. 1 Corinthians 6:20

I am a member of Christ's Body
Now you are the body of Christ, and each one of you is a part of it. 1 Corinthians 12:27

I am a Saint
Paul, an apostle of Christ Jesus, by the will of God, to the saints in Ephesus, the faithful in Christ Jesus: Ephesians 1:1

I have been adopted as God's child
...he predestined us to be adopted as his sons through Jesus Christ, in accordance with his pleasure and will... Ephesians 1:5

I have direct access to God through his Holy Spirit
For through him we both have access to the Father by one Spirit. Ephesians 2:18

I have been redeemed and forgiven of all my sins

...in whom we have redemption, the forgiveness of sins. Colossians 1:14

I am complete in Christ
...and you have been given fullness in Christ, who is the Head of every power and authority. Colossians 2:10

I Am Secure in Christ
I am free forever from condemnation.
Therefore there is no condemnation for those who are in Christ Jesus, because through Christ Jesus the law of the Spirit of life set me free from the law of sin and death. Romans 8:1,2

I am assured that all things work together for good.
And we know that in all things God works for good of those who love him, who have been called according to his purpose. Romans 8:28

I am free from any condemning charges against me.
Who will bring any charge against those whom God has chosen? It is God who justifies. Who is he that condemns? Christ Jesus, who died- more than that, who was raised to life – is at the right hand of God and also interceding for us. Romans 8:33, 34

I cannot be separated from the love of God.
Who shall separate us from the love of Christ? Shall trouble or hardship or persecution or famine or nakedness or danger or sword? Romans 8:35

I have been established, anointed and sealed by God.
Now it is God who makes us and you stand firm in Christ.

He anointed us, set his seal of ownership on us, and put his Spirit in our hearts as a deposit, guaranteeing what is to come. 2 Corinthians 1:21,22

I am hidden with Christ in God.
For you died, and your life is now hidden with Christ in God. Colossians 3:3

I am confident that the good work God has began in me will be perfected.
…being confident of this, that he who begun a good work in you will carry it on to completion until the day of Christ Jesus. Philippians 1:6

I am a citizen of heaven.
But our citizenship is in heaven. And we eagerly await a saviour from there, the Lord Jesus Christ. Philippians 3:20

I have not been given a spirit of fear, but of power, love and sound mind.
For God did not give us a spirit of timidity, but a spirit of power, of love and of self-discipline. 2 Timothy 1:7

I can find grace and mercy in time of need.
Let us then approach the throne of grace with confidence, so that we may receive mercy and find grace to help in our time of need. Hebrews 4:16

I am born of God and the evil one cannot touch me.
We know that anyone born of God does not continue to sin; the one who was born of God keeps him safe, and the evil one cannot harm him. 1John 5:18

I Am Significant in Christ

I am the salt and light of the earth.
You are the salt of the earth. But if the salt loses its saltiness, how can it be made salty again? It is no longer good for anything, except to be thrown out and trampled by men. You are the light of the world. A city on a hill cannot be hidden. Matthew 5:13,14

I am a branch of the true vine, a channel of his life.
I am the true vine, and my Father is the gardener. I am the vine; you are the branches. If a man remains in me and I in him, he will bear much fruit; apart from me you can do nothing. John 15:1,5

I have been chosen and appointed to bear fruit.
You did not choose me, but I chose you and appointed you to go and bear fruit - fruit that will last. Then the Father will give you whatever you ask in my name. John 15:16

I am a personal witness of Christ.
But you will receive power when the Holy Spirit comes on you; and you will be my witnesses in Jerusalem, and in all Judea and Samaria, and to the ends of the earth. Acts 1:8

I am God's temple.
Don't you know that you yourselves are God's Temple and that God's Spirit lives in you? 1 Corinthians 3:16

I am a minister of reconciliation.
Therefore, if anyone is in Christ, he is a new creation; the old has

gone the new has come! All this is from God, who reconciled us to himself through Christ and gave us the ministry of reconciliation: that God was reconciling the world to himself in Christ, not counting men's sins against them and has committed to us the message of reconciliation. We are therefore Christ ambassadors, as though God were making his appeal through us. We implore you on Christ behalf: Be reconciled to God. 2 Corinthians 5:17-20

I am God's coworker.
As God's fellow-workers we urge you not to receive God's grace in vain. 2 Corinthians 6:1

I am seated with Christ in the heavenly realm.
And God raised us up with Christ and seated us with him in the heavenly realms in Christ Jesus… Ephesians 2:6

I am God's workmanship.
For we are God's workmanship, created in Christ Jesus to do good works, which God prepared in advance for us to do. Ephesians 2:10

I may approach God with freedom and confidence.
In him and through faith in him we may approach God with freedom and confidence. Ephesians 3:12

I can do all things through Christ who strengthens me.
I can do everything through him who gives me strength. Philippians 4:13

Prayer

Chapter 7
FUNDAMENTAL PRAYER TOPICS

These are some prayer topics that will be of tremendous help to you on your threshing floor to serve as a solid foundation for your future. You must remember that as you pray you must bring God into remembrance of his Word, so use these prayer topics as the Holy Spirit leads and directs you in prayer.

Praying for exams success

Prov. 2:2   Grace to listen, concentrate and understand.

Jas 1:5   When you need wisdom to study the right materials.

Ps 16:7   Divine direction

Jer 33:3   Other areas you needs to study as well

Is 20:21 Direction of the Holy Spirit Prov.

2:6-7 Knowledge and understanding

1Jn 2:27   The Holy Spirit to teach you.

Prayer to know your purpose in life.

Matt. 1:21, Jer 1:4-5	Message of purpose in life
Prov. 16:9	The Lord's direction
Prov. 19:21	The Lord's purpose to prevail
Prov. 15:22, 8:8	Good advices that are in line with God's purpose for you.
Ps 138:8	The Lord's will of his plan in your life.
Isa 42: 9	The Lord to tell you the future.

Prayer for all around success

Ps 1:1-3	What you do to prosper
Job 22:26 -28	Whatever you decide to be accomplished
Isa 30:23	Rains on your labour
Ps 112:1-3	Wealth and riches in your house
Deut. 28:1-13	Blessing
Deut. 11:13-15	Plenty to eat
Phil 4:18-19	All your needs to be supplied
Is.65:21-24	Time to enjoy fruit of your labour
Ps 128	Happiness
Eph 3:20	Exceedingly above your thinking or asking

Prayer for a job or ideas to create jobs

Jer.33:3	Asking God
Jas 1:5	Wisdom to create
Eph 3:20	Creative thinking
Isa 30:7, 15	Ideas for productivity or productive ideas
Isa 30:21	Direction
Ps 112:5	Discretion

Prayer for the nations

1 Tim 2:1-2	Salvation, peace quietness godliness and dignity
Pro 28:2	Wise and knowledgeable leaders
Prov. 16:12, 14:13	Righteousness
Isa 66:12, Rom 14:17, Isa 60:17	Peace
Isa 54:14	Just and fair government
Isa 60	No violence, desolation or destruction.

Prayer for your husband

Eph 5:22-23	Love towards wife and children.
Jer 31:32	No divorce
1 Pet 3:7	To give honour to wife
1 Cor 7:5	No sexual deprivation
1 Cor 7:11	Cannot but stay with wife
Prov. 31:11	Trust the wife
Prov. 31:23	Well known with influence
Prov. 31:28	Praise wife
Prov. 12 :14	Enjoy benefits of work
Ps 128:1	Rich & happy
Ps 128:6	Love to enjoy grandchildren
1 Tim. 3:2	Faithful, one who exhibit self control, enjoy guest, gift of teaching, control, live wisely, good reputation.

Prayer for your wife

Titus 2: 4-5	Love for husband, children,take care of the home and submission.
1Pet 3:1	Godly life
1Cor 7:5, Rom 5:15	No sexual deprivation.
1Cor 7:11	Cannot but stay with husband
Ps 128: 3, 16	Faithfulness, live to enjoy grandchildren

Prov. 12:4	Worthy wife.
Prov. 15:17	Someone you love
Prov. 31:10	Virtuous and capable wife.
Prov. 31:30	A wife who fears God
Gen. 12:3	Through her families will be blessed
Deut 28:11, Ex 2:2	Children.

Prayer for your children

Gen 33:3	Given by God
Eph 6:1	Obedience
1Cor 17:14	Godly influence
Ps 128:3	Vigorous and healthy
Prov. 22:15, 29:15	Love corrections
Luke 2:52	To grow in wisdom and stature
Matt 1:21	Children of purpose
Eph 5:8-9	Children of light
Ps 112:2	To be successful everywhere

BIBLIOGRAPHY

Brain Tracy and Andrew Wood, Dream Big Dreams (Publishing Press, 2000)

Bruce Wilkinson, Secrets of the Vine (USA: Multnomah Publishers Inc, 2001)

Colin Urguhart, The Great Revelation (Published by Integrity media Europe, 2009)

Dag Heward-Mills, Demons and how to deal with them (Parchment House, 2005)

Max Lucado, On the Anvil (Tyndale House Publishing, Inc, 2005)

Neil T Anderson and Rich Miller, Walking in Freedom (USA: Published by regal books, 1999) p 205